The Beginner's Guide to Making a Profit with Chickens, Ducks or Quail

Other books by Tammie Cappuccio

The Beginner's Guide to Hatching Chicken Eggs

The Beginner's Guide to Hatching Quail Eggs

The Teen Years: Ways to Connect With Your Teen

Note to Readers:

This book was put together to help anyone, with any sized farm, make a profit raising poultry (specifically with chickens, ducks and/or quail). The key is diversity. You'll succeed if you can do many of the topics well.

To navigate the book with ease, it is set up into sections, as you can see, in the table of contents. Within each chapter, the topics are set up alphabetically. Hopefully, this will make the book easy to read, and easy to go back to selected topics when needed.

If you have come up with something not listed in this book, please share with me at my email address, cspots@netzero.net.

Happy Reading!

Table of Contents

Chapter 1: Butchering and It's Profits

A freshly butchered chicken

Butchering a chicken, duck or quail

Butchering your birds gives you two ways you can make a profit. One way is to butcher your birds to sell to the public directly by offering whole birds butchered and ready to cook. Another way is to make yourself available to offer pre-cooked meals, using your birds, to busy families that may not have time to cook. Offering to butcher other people's birds is another way to make some money.

Raising your birds from chicks and ducklings and growing them out to butchering time provides, not only for yourself but the ability to offer your butchered poultry directly to the public. Many states have exemptions to their farm animal regulations that allow anyone to butcher their birds. Some states will have regulations on how you can sell them at farmer's markets and to restaurants.

Check on your regulations in your state before offering to sell at these venues.

Once you have researched your state's regulations, and if you find you can sell directly to the consumer, this can offer you a good outlet to be able to market your chickens, ducks or quail. You can build up a customer base directly from your farm, or sell directly to restaurants. Talk to potential customers to give you an idea of how many birds you should butcher. Start small at first and if you are successful, butcher more the next time. Let people put in orders beforehand. The more time that goes by, the more the public will get to know you. Word of mouth will get more potential customers interested in what you have. The sooner you start letting people know who you are and what you have to offer, the quicker you can see profits in your business or farm.

When to Butcher a Chicken, Duck or Quail

There are some basic breeds of chicken, ducks and quail that are typically used for eating. The age of the bird at butchering time is important for the flavor and texture of the meat. The time to butcher will vary depending on if it is a meat bird or a dual purpose bird. A typical meat bird for a chicken would be a Cornish or Cornish cross. A dual purpose chicken could be a Rhode Island Red or a Sussex for example. Pekin ducks are a popular meat bird, and the Jumbo Coturnix quail are known for their tasty meat.

The Cornish or Cornish cross would be ready at about eight weeks old at 4 lbs. A dual purpose bird would be 16 weeks and 4-6 lbs. If you wait too long, meat birds may have health issues, and the meat gets tougher (good for soup). A Pekin duck is typically butchered at 7-8 weeks and a quail at 8-10 weeks. Also, keep in mind that the longer you feed your young birds, the costlier it is to raise them to butcher weight.

How to Butcher Poultry

Butchering a chicken, duck or quail is fairly straight forward. To start, you want to be able to keep the bird calm during the butchering process. For chickens, there are various methods to use such as using a kill cone or sack. These will keep you from the sight of a headless chicken or duck running around by holding the body calmly during the procedure.

A kill cone can be fashioned out of old traffic cones with the end cut off. If you don't have a cone, a gallon plastic jug with the spout area enlarged enough for the chicken's head will work. Cones are typically nailed to a tree or other upright, strong surface so that the container or cone will hold the bird upside down with the head sticking out of the bottom. The easiest way to put the chicken in the cone is to hold them by their legs, upside down. They typically calm down in this position. Fold the wings against the body and insert into the cone.

Using a very sharp knife, you hold the head in one hand and use the knife to make a deep cut from just behind one earlobe to just behind the other. Use very strong pressure as you need to get through the feathers. Some people only cut one side (cutting one artery), and therefore not hitting the windpipe, but they will "go to sleep" faster if both arteries are cut. Once cut it takes 30 seconds to a minute for the chicken to die. Let the chicken bleed out and they will become unconscious and the life will flow out of them. Some people choose just to cut the head right off. This can be done, but you must have a very sharp knife capable of cutting through the spine. Cutting the head off is better if you use a killing block. You can use a tree stump or other hard, flat surface that you can use an ax to cut clean through the neck. This can be a hit or miss unless you are experienced and might cause the chicken unneeded distress and pain. You can put in two nails that will hold the chickens head straight and pull the body taunt so the neck stretches out and can't move. Use a sharp ax to quickly and cleanly sever the head. You'll want to have the chicken in a sack with the head sticking out so it will not go running around, literally, with its head cut off. Some people will not use a sack and will chop the head off with an ax and hang the bird up to drain out. Stand back, though, because the nerves in the bird do make them thrash around after the head is cut off.

For ducks use a cloth or gunny sack. While holding the duck with the wings at its side, slip it into the sack with the head sticking out a corner that you have cut out of the sack. You can use an ax to chop off the head. You can also using a very sharp knife (the same as described above for chickens), to cut both sides of the duck's neck and then let the blood drain into a bucket.

You can also use a small kill cone for quail. Quail are smaller and a very sharp pair of kitchen shears will cleanly cut the head off. You can then hang the bird to let the blood drain out.

Butchering for others (they bring their birds to you)

Many people would like to raise their birds for meat. They raise their birds on pasture or in a coop and when the time comes to process the birds they look for someone to do the processing for them. This is where you come in. You can offer your services and charge them a price per bird. You can have them bring the birds to you, or you can have a mobile processing trailer. You can offer standard butchering where they will do the processing after you have killed the birds. Or you could offer to do the whole process.

A Freshly Processed and frozen duck

Processing a Bird for Human Consumption

After butchering your chicken, duck or quail by one of the methods above you can get to the next step: scalding.

After butchering and bleeding out the carcass, dip the bird into a large pot of water at 145-150 degrees for 3 seconds and shake it gently while submerged. Take the bird from the water, wait a short moment and dunk again for 3 seconds. Do this a total of 3 times then try pulling a feather out. If it comes out easily, you're ready for the next step. If it still has some resistance continue the 3-second dunks until they come free easily. Ducks should be left in the water for a longer period as it is tougher to get the feathers loosened than a chicken. Instead of holding the duck under the water for 3 seconds, hold it for 6 seconds, and then try pulling a feather. Quails go through the same process. Hold and dunk for the 3 seconds and if it doesn't seem to be coming loose, leave the quail under the water for a longer period.

Plucking is the next step after scalding. You can pick feathers by hand, you can use a manufactured plucker, or you can make your own plucker. Searching the internet for "homemade chicken plucker" will bring up easy-to-do plans. Picking feathers by hand is time-consuming but can be done for a few birds but if you have a large amount you may want to invest or make your own plucker.

With the plucker, place the bird after it's been scalded into the plucker. Turn the machine on and while you spray the bird with water the machine will do its job. You want to keep the water on it to wash away the small feathers that like to stick to the skin.

Once your bird is plucked, you are now ready to do the cleaning of the bird.

With cleaning, you need a sharp knife. You will remove the feet, guts, and head. You want to remove the feet and legs at the joint that connects the leg to the foot. Insert you knife right in the middle of the joint, and it should separate fairly easily. A filet knife works well here.

To remove the head, pruners work best. The spine can be difficult to cut through, so a sharp set of pruners is needed. Once you cut through the spine the rest is fairly easy to cut through.

To remove the innards put the bird on its back, so the breast is on top. Slit the skin at the narrow end of the breast. Gently open up the bird, so the body cavity is revealed. Reach into the cavity and pull out all the guts. Be careful as you don't want to rupture the intestines as it will contaminate the bird.

When taking the guts out, the windpipe will get in the way. It is a long straw-like thing at the top of the cavity. You'll need to pull this out using some strength as its tough. When you are finished pulling that and the other innards out the cavity, the cavity should be empty. You need a sharp filet knife to cut around the vent to separate the intestines from the carcass. The rest should all come out freely.

Lastly place the chicken in a bucket of ice. It should stay in the ice until you are finished butchering all the birds. There are many videos out there that show the whole process if you were interested in visuals as well as reading the instructions.

To preserve the bird for later cooking, wash the bird inside and out. Make sure all the feathers are off, and everything looks clean and place in a shrink wrap bag (don't close it yet). Some people may want the innards or other parts so they can be placed an individual shrink-wrapped bag.

Place the bird and extras into the refrigerator for a day or two. The bag should be open at this point. This will allow the chicken to be pliable and not get stiff and chewy. This results in a much more tender bird. After two days finish shrink wrapping your bird, so they are ready for the freezer.

The customer/owner can pick up the birds at this point to put them in their freezer. You can freeze them first, if you have the freezer space, and give the birds already frozen to your customer.

Mobile butchering trailer

A mobile butchering trailer can be a useful method for making money and can be used for you to butcher birds at different locations. You will need a trailer that you can store and move your butchering equipment from place to place. You make arrangements to set up for a day or couple of days. Choose a location where local people can bring their birds to you to be butchered, which they can take home after you butcher their birds. As an alternative for a larger farm, you can arrange to go farm to farm. Typically you could charge a flat rate to come out to the farm and then a price per bird. You will want to do some figuring of finances beforehand to see if this is an economical option for you. You need to factor in wear and tear on your machinery, gas and your time. You can use a generator, or you can contract to use the farm's electricity. You also may need a permit and have regulations regarding food, so check with your local town hall to see what may be required.

Another option of the mobile butcher is to rent your unit to farmers to butcher their birds. They can come to your farm with their truck and hook up to your mobile unit and haul it to their farm to use. You can charge a per-day or per-bird basis.

Rules, regulations and permitting vary state to state. Check with your local health official to obtain what is required to operate or rent out a mobile butchering unit before investing any money into buying equipment, to see if it is something you can make a profit on.

Supplier for animal organizations such as zoos or rehab centers.

Being a supplier for animal organizationsss such as zoos or rehab centers is a small niche market that may bring you some small income or large income- the sky is the limit! If you are a large farm with lots of chickens, you can supply a wide range of zoos if you can freeze larger quantities of birds. Chicken is usually the bird of choice. Contact your local zoo and ask where they get their chickens. If you can supply a better product (drug free, free range, cut a certain way, for example) and offer a good price, you may get the contract to supply them with a regular supply of chickens. This has the potential to expand to other zoos, which are not in your area if you can offer shipping of frozen chickens.

Human consumption (supply directly to the public)

Farmer's markets have been popping up all over. These groups allow local farms to supply their product directly to the public. Contact your local farmer's market and check to see if selling butchered poultry is allowed. It will vary market to market and state rules will be different state to state. A Farmer's market may allow you to sell butchered fresh or frozen chickens to the public. It would also give you the opportunity for the public to meet you and learn about your fresh chickens, ducks, and quail. You can put together a list of people that would like fresh or frozen birds either delivered to them or picked up at your farm on a weekly basis. You can charge a small fee for delivery.

People are becoming more and more interested in the better cared for and drug-free product for their families. As a farmer, you can offer this kind of product for them directly from the farm. Many people have said that a chicken raised in a humane way and drug-free is worth the extra cost over a big store bought chicken. Being good at speaking with the public will go far in selling you, as the farmer, as an honest, humane and worthwhile source of their family's food.

Chapter 2: Feathers

Adam's Dry Fly

Lures and Capes for Fly Fishing

Fly fishing is a popular hobby. This hobby has the potential to make some profit with the use of chicken feathers. You can sell flies that you make, or you can sell hackle and saddle feathers called "capes." If you butcher your birds, you can sell the feathers. Prices are good at an average of $50 for a premium cape from a rooster. Hen feathers bring a bit less at an average of $25 per cape.

Fly fishing is a method of fishing that involves using man-made lures out of various materials. There are two kinds of flies- dry and wet. Dry flies are made using materials that cause the lure to float, and the wet fly is that which is set under the water.

Many different kinds of materials are used to create the fly. Feathers are often used. You can buy flies or make them yourself to use or make them to sell. If you can produce a quality product, you can get a good price for your flies (called fly-tying).

Learning to tie flies is fairly straightforward and is typically a step-by-step process. When you have learned to tie your flies, it should take you 5 to 10 minutes to tie a fly. There are fly-tying kits available that will have everything you need. You can also learn from someone that already is a master of the craft. There are websites available that also will show you how to tie flies as well as videos online. Many books are also available. Many of the larger stores that have a fly fishing department will hold regular classes where you can learn to tie flies.

Some of the items you'll need in your kit:

VARIOUS FEATHERS, TINSELS, SILKS, FURS, AND HOOKS. These can be purchased from a store that specializes in fishing or online. The better quality materials you buy, the better product your finished fly will be.

NEEDLE. You'll need a needle to clear the excess cement from your fly and releasing materials that may accidentally get tied down by mistake.

VISE. A vise is a small clamp that is clamped to a table and will hold the hook firmly while you tie your fly. Don't go with the cheapest one you can find- go for a quality product because if your vise can't adequately hold the hook you'll never get your fly done.

HACKLE PLIERS. These are small spring-action forceps that are needed to twine the feathers around the hook.

BOBBIN. You don't want to be without this little gadget that holds down the tying silk as you work on your fly. Beginners, in particular, will find this tool helpful.

SCISSORS. You should have two pairs. One small pair and one about 3 ½" long. They should both taper to a fine point.

FLY-TYING WAX. Buying pre-waxed tying silk saves you a step. If you buy the tying silk without wax, you will need to coat it with fly-tying wax.

FLY-TYING CEMENT. Fly-tying cement is necessary to hold your various materials together.

Kits are popular if you are a beginner. If you buy a kit, it should have everything you need in one kit. Kits can range from $25 up to $60 depending on if the kit also includes the feathers, fur, tinsel and other materials on just includes the basic tools. Many will also come with a DVD.

Feathers: Selling your flies

There are many outlets for selling your flies as well as your feather capes. To determine price, check out online stores and sites. Check out your local fishing store and see what they are charging. To start out, you may want to price your flies and capes less than your competition. As you see your product selling well, you could consider charging more. Realistically, expect to get from $7-$10 per dozen for flies.

You can approach different fly-tying specialty stores or sell direct to the customers online from your own website or on one of the auction sites. Social media outlets are ways to connect with the fly-tying world.

Another outlet is to produce flies for decorative purposes. It's with the decorative purposes that you can let your creative talent come up with some interesting uses for your feathers for the flies. You can make a lure into a tiepin, cufflinks, embed them in clear plastic as paperweights, glue finished flies to picture frames, among other things.

If you can get a customer base or selling outlet (like online), you can make some money tying flies and using the feathers from your own birds as well as making doodads like paperweights as well. You can sell your flies as well as capes. This not only can turn from a fun and relaxing hobby, but it's a nice way to pick up some extra dollars!

Feathers: Other crafts

Many crafts can be made from feathers and sold. Dreamcatchers are an item you can make with a minimal amount of material and your chicken, duck or quail feathers. You could also set up a booth at local fairs. Parents would pay a small fee for their child to be given their choice of materials (like feathers) and glue them onto such items as plastic cups, felt or construction paper cutouts and egg cartons to name a few. This hands-on craft project is very popular with the young children. Other crafts include making and selling hair accessories, necklaces, bracelets, pins and other like projects.

A feathered hat from
Etsy.com/shop/alicehartcouture

Feathers: Milliner

Ladies hats are popular with colorful and attractive feathers. Finding a Milliner could be an outlet to sell those longer more colorful feathers- particularly of the rooster tails.

Chapter 3: Eggs

Egg Candles from Etsy.com/shops/TinkrGems

There are lots of uses for the eggs of our featured poultry. From eating to various crafts, there are lots of fun things to do with eggs.

Egg blowing- the basics for your egg shell crafts

There are many crafts available using egg shells. The first start in these projects is to get a clean and empty eggshell. Follow the directions below to get your eggs ready for your crafts.

Blow out your fresh egg by making a hole in the bottom and the top of the egg. Using a needle or other implement (a crochet hook works great) break the yolk and mix the white and the yolk in the eggshell. Blow on one end and the yolk and white should come out the other hole. You can also make just one hole and use a syringe (without the needle).

After emptying, wash out with warm soapy water, rinse and allow to dry. You can microwave the shells for ten seconds to get rid of any germs that may be on the shell.

Egg Candles

You can make these at home and sell at local crafts fairs.

What you need: crayons, leftover white candles, can for melting wax, blown out eggshell, wick, water, pan, egg carton, hairdryer, play doh.

See egg blowing at the beginning of this chapter.

When you have your empty and clean egg shell, thread a wick through the egg and hold it in place on the bottom with play doh, effectively sealing the large end of the egg. Set the eggshell into an egg carton with the small end up or on a piece of wax paper.

Place a can in boiling water and melt the leftover white candles. Add 1/3 to ½ of a crayon into the can to melt and mix. Using only one color works best as you don't get the best results mixing two or more colors. Keep the can in the boiling water until the wax and crayon are liquid.

Make sure you have a fairly large hole in the top of the egg so you can pour in the melted crayons. Pour in until the wax is ¼ full and let it cool and harden. Repeat this until the egg is full. As it cools the wax shrinks so you will have a dip in the wax each time you add to it, and it cools. Once topped off let it cool completely.

Peel the eggshell off and use a hair dryer to smooth any rough edges. Warm the bottom of the candle with the hairdryer or by placing the bottom of the candle on the cans warm pot to flatten the bottom so it will be easy to have it stand on its own.

Voila! A fun Easter project or for anytime!

Egg carton crafts

Children love to do hands-on projects and parents would gladly pay a ticket if you had a booth at a fair, to watch their children enjoy themselves.

Egg carton crafts make a great crafts fair exhibit. Set out egg cartons, safety scissors, tempera paints, craft glue, wiggly eyes, tissue paper, pipe cleaners, feathers, felt and anything you can think of that a child would like to decorate their egg carton with.

The children will delight in making their project, parents will be happy, and you can pocket the value of the ticket.

Cute egg crafts – Simplethingssweetlife.blogspot.com

Egg decorating

Have an egg decorating party or set up a booth at the craft fair. Parents would delight in having something where their child could participate.

This idea works great as an activity at a fair. The kids love making their egg-projects!

What you need: glue, blown eggshells, craft supplies like felt, feathers, wiggly eyes, tissue paper, pipe cleaners, etc.

See the egg blowing at the beginning of this chapter to start with clean empty eggshells.

Using blown eggs, apply glue and decorate to your taste! Cute little creatures or fun designs- whatever suits your fancy.

Hand Carved Pysanka Egg-photo by
Ebay seller Soloveiko.Inc

Eggshell carving

This hobby has been quite active as an adult activity. Crafters will pay for blown out white or light-colored eggs of good shape and in different sizes.

It is typical to use a Dremel like tool to do the carving. The Dremel has many carving tips that can be used for different effects. Well done examples can bring good prices.

Crafters can be seen at online auctions like Ebay or have a shop on Etsy. Both places allow you to sell your eggs directly to the public. You would collect your eggs, blow them out (see beginning of the chapter), let them dry and organize them by size and color. Offer them in groups of half a dozen, a dozen or 18 eggs. Check current prices of other sellers to get an idea of how you should price yours. You can also join eggshell carving or crafts groups to sell your eggs too.

Egg Soap for kids

These also make something parents will pay a small price for just to get their kids more interested in washing!

This craft can encourage kids to want to use soap and wash!

What you need: Melt and Pour soap (available online or in a craft store), blown eggshells, small plastic dinosaurs or other animals, egg carton, play doh.

See how to blow out eggs at the beginning of this chapter.

Start with a blown out eggshell (see egg blowing above) and make the hole at the small end large enough to fit in your small plastic toy. Plug the other end with play doh and set in the egg carton. Warm your Melt & Pour soap according to directions and pour into the egg.

Put the carton into the refrigerator to harden. When cool, break off the eggshell (a knife might work well here). The surface will be a little rough but will smooth out with a first few uses.

Now you have soap that kids will love to use to get to the toy dinosaur or another animal inside.

Farmers Market – Franklin, MA

Eggs and more to sell at Farmer's Markets

Many towns now hold Farmer's Markets where local farmers or growers bring the foods they produce to sell directly to the public. Farmer's Markets are a good place to find fresh produce and eggs. This is a popular route for many people who have chickens and want to sell the eggs. Often this is a weekly event.

You can set up a booth and sell your eggs. You may also be able to sell live chickens, and chicken already butchered. Ethnic communities, in particular, will buy live chickens to take home and butcher. If you attend regularly, you can get a customer base that will pre-order and pick up at the market.

Each Farmer's market will have its county and market rules about this so check beforehand.

Duck, chicken and quail eggs

Eggs to sell to others

If you have a regular supply of eggs that you can count on weekly, you can sell your eggs from your home. Many people like the idea of a fresh egg. People will get to know you and order for a weekly pick up or delivery. You can offer samples to prospective buyers. Prices vary according to where you live. Check with others who sell eggs in your area for a comparison.

You could set up a delivery service and charge a small fee. Buyers will appreciate the extra service.

Eggs to sell to restaurants

Restaurants often like to get their supplies locally. If you have a large steady supply of eggs, approach local establishments and offer them free samples of your eggs. If you are a very large operation, you could even offer to supply chicken. Start up a relationship with the establishment owners and they just may take your business.

Feed eggs back to birds and make your own supplement

Produce your own egg supplement to sell to caged birders. Cooked eggs are often used as egg food for young birds or to add protein to the diet.

Create your own market for this egg-food. Poultry also like cooked eggs and would enjoy them for a treat.

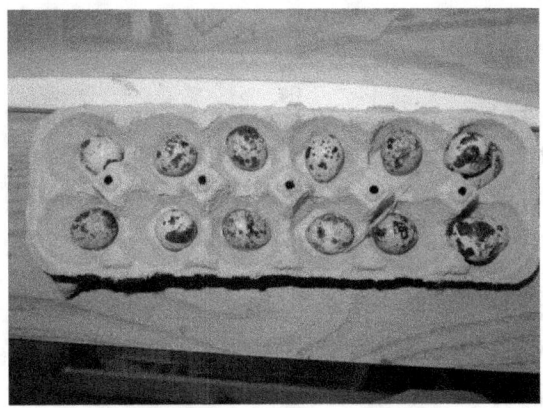

Fertile Coturnix Quail eggs

Fertile Hatching eggs to sell

If you have a rooster and hens (or a drake and ducks) of the same breed, you can sell fertile hatching eggs. Hatching eggs are eggs you sell to other people for them to hatch. You can also sell a "barnyard mix" if you don't have pure breeds.

Open up the first batch of eggs to make sure they are fertile. If they are fertile, you will see a small white bulls-eye on the yolk. You can sell them so buyers come right to your farm, or you can sell them online at different sites that sell poultry eggs like Ebay and backyardchickens.com.

You can also advertise at your local feed stores and put up fliers at chicken related events.

When you are planning on selling fertile eggs, you will collect the eggs each day. They should be kept small side down in a cool place. After gathering the eggs for up to a week, they are ready to put in the incubator or sell to others to incubate. If you are going to sell online you can estimate when you'll have half dozen or a dozen eggs and set up an auction to end just as the eggs are ready to be shipped to the auction winner.

Sending eggs through the mail is common. The easiest way is to use the United States Post Office free Priority boxes. There are various ways to pack fertile eggs: individually in packing peanuts, in an egg carton with fill such as peanuts, shredded newspaper or other materials, or a very reliable way is with foam. Foam is typically the size of the box you are shipping in with small holes cut out to fit the eggs in with a foam pad on top and bottom. Whichever way you choose, you should have plenty of space and not jam the eggs in as they will be more easily broken.

You can set up a PayPal account and have your auction sales directly deposited into your account. Using PayPal will also allow you to buy your postage right online at a discount when shipping the eggs out.

Chapter 4: Coops/Henhouses/Runs

The Author's backyard coop

Build coops

Many people get into chickens, ducks or quail and are not handy enough to build their own coops. This is where you come in if you are handy working with wood and power tools. You can start by building a few coops and selling them online or putting up fliers at feed stores. Start out by building a henhouse for 4-6 chickens so people can see your work. You can offer just the coop or add an attached run. A common size henhouse would be 4' long x 3' high by 2' deep. You will want to have a roosting pole and one or two nest boxes. You'll need a window for ventilation, a ramp and a door that can be securely closed at night. For six hens, you'll want at least a 6' x 6' run. Many, many examples can be found on the internet. You can browse for different styles and sizes.

You can start out by making at least one of a henhouse/run combination to show prospective clients. You can put ads and fliers out at auctions, feed stores, online and local papers. Talk to feed stores that sell chicken products but don't have coops and work out a deal so that both of you can benefit by selling your coops at the store.

You could start smaller and make a coop that is portable so you could bring it to swaps, farm or chicken sales, and fairs. Offer to take orders for custom coops. Add delivery free as a bonus or make delivery available for a small fee.

For large coops, offer to go to their location and build the coop they request. Sometimes this might be refurbishing an older building or making a corner of a barn suitable to hold chickens. One option is to buy one of the wooden sheds you can get as a kit from the big box stores and adding whatever is needed to make it a nice chicken house and add a large run.

Some people may only need a henhouse. If you are good at following plans, there are thousands of coop plans available online. Many are free and available for you to download or you can buy a book with an unlimited number of plans for a small cost. Auction sites often have these available.

Building coops are a way to make some good money. Be fair in your pricing and don't shortchange yourself.

Chicken tractor made by the author

Build tractors

Along the lines of building coops is building chicken tractors. They are called "chicken" tractors, but they can house any poultry. These tractors are small portable coops that have wheels and can be moved from place to place. They are typically very simple in design with lots of examples available online and in books. They typically consist of a small area for them to get out of the weather and an area for them to get out in the sun and grass or garden with an open bottom. This allows the birds some natural behaviors such as digging and scratching and some turning of the soil in the garden in the case of chickens and quails. Some tractors can be small, to house only 3-4 hens, while supervised in the yard or garden. This type would not have a shelter attached so the weather would have to be watched to make sure they can be brought in for shelter in bad weather.

Tractors are also great for a mother hen and her chicks as well as a duck and her ducklings. The tractor need not be very large- a standard sized hen with a half dozen chicks could easily enjoy a 2' x 4' tractor that is moved every day. This way they get fresh air and sunshine and they can dig and scratch if they like, and still be protected.

Tractors are typically very basic and easy to put together. Costs tend to be minimal with the wheels being the biggest expense unless you can find an inexpensive supply of used lawn mowers and repurpose those for your tractor. As with most things being hand built, you can take custom orders for tractors. There is quite the profit to be made with building and selling chicken tractors.

Coop cleaning service & coop poop collection service

Many people dread the thought of having to clean out the coop. This is where you can come in and make some money. There are two schools of thought when it comes so coop cleaning- the deep litter method and the regular cleaning method.

The deep litter method is where the first layer in the hen house is shavings, hay, pine needles, moss, leaves or some material that will disintegrate. Regularly the top layer of the bedding is cleaned out of chicken manure. Some people don't clean out at all except for once or twice a year. Each week a new layer of clean bedding is put down on top of the old bedding. As the bedding composts, it creates heat and gives the chickens a place to scratch around. Often this type of method will be cleaned out in spring and fall or just in the fall.

The regular method is to clean the coop regularly and remove the chicken manure. This can be made easier by using poop boards that catch the manure as it's expelled. Chickens expel manure the majority of the time at night, and the boards are easily cleaned weekly.

You can be hired to do the once a year clean out and either compost on the property or remove the compost. Compost made out of chicken poop is highly desired in the garden, and you can pile any you take away and sell it.

You can also hire yourself out to do weekly or bi-weekly cleanings.

Quail are often in wire floored housing, so the manure falls through. Underneath still has to be cleaned up on a regular basis, so the fly population is kept down as well as the smell. Ducks may need their yard raked of manure and duck houses cleaned out.

Some people would rather hire someone to clean the coops either because they choose not to, have allergies, or don't have the time. No matter what the reason, this gives you the opportunity to make some money with the potential to make even more by selling what you clean out.

Draw up or collect hen house plans to sell

There are dozens, if not hundreds, of plans being made available on the internet for free. You could collect those plans into a book and offer the book for sale (or disc). This is done quite a bit with free items that are available-someone comes along that will gather the free items together and sell them as a package or group. It costs very little to nothing but your time.

Look up the search engines for "free henhouse plans, free coop plans, free chicken coop plans," etc. Organize them by type. Make sure you are not infringing on copyrights when you gather your plans. Use one of the free book publishing services online that lets you self- publish. As an alternative to self-publishing, you could load the plans onto a disc and sell the disc.

With the whole process free you have the opportunity to make some money selling plans to chicken owners.

Chapter 5:
Exhibits/Shows/Swaps/Fairs/Workshops

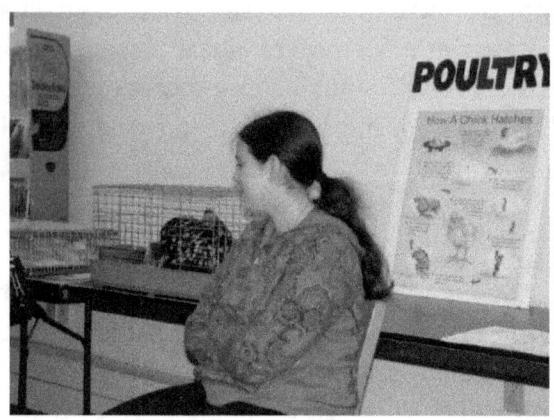

Melyssa Cappuccio giving a demonstration

Exhibits/Presentations

Exhibits and presentations can offer some fun along with earning some money. Exhibiting/presenting your birds to the public tends to be well received. You can offer to bring your birds to Boy Scout meetings, 4-H, and Future Farmers of America, schools, clubs, farm days, fairs and libraries. There are many avenues to show the public your chickens, ducks or quail that are not mentioned here. Find out the contacts of these groups and offer your services. You can charge a fee, or you can donate your time. If you donate your time, you can give out business cards or fliers so that if the people you're presenting to want poultry later on, they will have you as a contact.

You can advertise in local papers, fliers, online, club newsletters or contact people directly by phone.

One example you could do is to bring a few chickens for people to see in person (some people have never seen a chicken in person). Use a carrier that is made so you can see the chicken well. A small guinea pig cage works well for this. Standing beside your chickens (and you can even be holding one if you like) you can tell some basic facts about chickens. For presentations to young children, you could read a book featuring a chicken. You can allow questions. Your time frame will depend on the specific event. For a Library visit, for instance, you wouldn't allow people to hold your chickens, especially if you are inside. A typical presentation might run 15 minutes for a short talk or half hour for a longer one.

These public appearances are a wonderful way to have the public learn about and meet live chickens. You'll want to make the best presentation you can by washing your chickens before the event, having clean cages and bedding and well-mannered chickens. If you get well known, you can make small tours in your local community.

Fairs (show and also buy and sell)

Fairs offer you a chance to show the public the type of birds you offer. Take your best birds and enter a fair. Fairs can be small town-run affairs or can be big weeks long country fairs. Fairs typically have agricultural classes for crop products as well as livestock and crafts. For the livestock, there will typically be classes for chickens, ducks, turkeys and sometimes quail. There may be 4-H classes or classes for Future Farmers of America to showcase their animals as well as open classes for everyone. Classes for chickens are popular and can also feature classes for egg production. Prices to enter are usually reasonable. Prizes can vary, from ribbons to prize money.

An agricultural fair often will have a sale of livestock. This is a chance for you and the 4-H or FFA kids to sell their animals. Some fairs have a sale barn. No matter what way the fair sets up so you can sell your animals it's a good source of potential customers.

Silkies after a successful show – photo by owner Stephanie Coli

Shows

Shows can be lots of fun and offer the opportunity to showcase some of your birds and also make some money.

Show fees are modest at typically, just a few dollars. A show will allow the public (potential buyers) as well as other chicken, duck or quail people, what kind of birds you have. Keeping fliers and business cards handy and out where they can be easily picked up is free advertising for you.

If you have some really good birds, you may be able to win some prizes- usually ribbons and sometimes prize money. One example of a recent large chicken show below:

The Northeastern Poultry Congress 2015 offered prizes for:

Champion trio $75 (rooster with two hens of the same breed, variety and age), 2nd place $50, 3rd $25

Display prizes champion $100, reserve $75, 3rd $50, 4th $35, 5th $25. A display consists of the same variety of birds and same breed. It requires five or more birds that shall be made up of not less than one entry in each of cock, hen, cockerel, pullet and trio classes. Awards are based on points accumulated individually.

Bird Raffles are a common and exciting event. If you donate a pair of birds, you qualify for winning a prize for getting the most tickets for your donated birds. The prize for this show was $25. Two raffles were held, one each day.

Cash awards were offered for (cash prize listed after the class):
Large chickens champion $75, Reserve $35, 3rd $25
Bantam Chickens champion $75, Reserve $35 and $25 3rd best
Waterfowl champion $75, Reserve $35, 3rd $25

Open classes:
Champion $ 25, Reserve $15

Champion in 4-H/Junior (10 birds or more must be in the class for cash awards to be given)
Champion $ 25, reserve $15,

Individual fancier's choice show specials (individual persons can opt to donate to sponsor a particular class) for example:

Best Cochin Bantam $10
Best Junior Bantam Cochin $5
Best Junior Nankin $5
Reserve Junior Nankin $5
Best Junior rose comb Nankin $5
Best Junior single comb Nankin $5
Best Junior Australorp $20
Best variety Silver Penciled Rock standard $15
Best variety Silver Penciled Rock Bantam $10
Best variety Silver Penciled Wyandotte LF $15
Reserve Silver Penciled Wyandotte LF $10
Best variety Splash Old English Game Bantam $10
Best non-Standard Color Plymouth Rock Bantam $10
Best display in Barred Rock Bantams $25

Shows also offer a chance to do some selling. Typically a 10 x 10 area to set up your sales birds is available. This is a good option if you have a lot of birds or bird related items to sell. A typical cost is $75. Coops are often rented individually if you only have a small number of birds. You must have a bird in the show to rent these spaces.

If you are showing a bird, you will be required to leave the bird in their coop until the show is over. This gives you a lot of time, and you will not want to be spending all day hanging around the sales area if you are renting coops there. Along with your sales bird's information, you should put your name and your phone number so prospective buyers can call you with questions, or ask you to come to the sales area so they can pay you. If you are renting a space you would want to be able to stay in your space most of the time as, hopefully, your space will be busy, and you'll be needed there to answer questions and sell your birds.

Swaps

Swaps are where like-minded people who have an interest in one particular thing get together to buy and sell their items. The swaps are open to the public as well. Typically a chicken swap will be held at a feed store or someone's farm. A date and time is set up, and fliers can be posted around town as well as listing the swap in local club news and poultry magazines as well as online.

Swaps are a great place to socialize. When there are some swaps in an area, you get to see familiar faces often. It's nice to be able to chat as well as sell some birds, eggs or other poultry. Most swaps will allow all types of poultry including chickens, turkeys, ducks and game birds. Some will even have raffles and an auction included.

A typical day would be to arrive at the swap half-hour before it is set to start. Find a spot near the center of the swap where there will be a lot of people looking. Bring some tables to set up your cages. Use cages that are clean and well-kept with fresh bedding. There usually is not electricity available, so if your chicks still need a heat lamp, you will want to bring a small, quiet generator. Set up your cages so that the birds are easy to see. If you can, bring a 10 x 10 canopy in case of rain or intense heat. Bring water for the birds and some feed for them. Be readily available in your spot to answer questions. Have a good amount of small bills available to make change and bring some empty boxes for buyers to bring their birds home in.

It's a good idea to bring some things for yourself as well such as a cooler and chairs. Have each of your cages marked with information such as the breed, age and gender of the birds. Some people will not buy if birds are not priced.

Be friendly and helpful, have a clean display and with a good location and advertising you should make some good sales.

Frank Schulenburg giving a presentation at Wikimania 2011

rkshops/Speaker

Workshops are a great way for the public to learn about chickens. Workshops can be held just about anywhere that has room to hold a small gathering.

Workshops are classes where you would make a presentation to people that are interested in a particular subject. They attend with the hopes of learning from you some information on a chosen subject. The subject can be anything and with poultry it could be topics such as basic care, different types of chickens, ducks or quail, chickens for pet therapy and much more. The sky is the limit when it comes to workshops.

Some workshops are free, but some speakers can charge a modest amount. Feed stores, in particular, may be willing to pay for you to come to the store and speak because they may offer chicks and poultry supplies. If you are talking about chicks and how to raise them the store may be able to make some money on selling chicks and supplies, so it's worth it to pay someone to come in and do a workshop- why not have it be you?

A workshop can be any length of time but should not be shorter than 20 minutes. Having brochures you can give out is helpful. Contact feed companies that the store stocks and see if they have brochures you can give out on feeds and supplies. Find out where the store got their chicks from and if they have any brochures that you can hand out. Some companies might send you coupons to give out. You can print fliers off of the internet (get permission first from the author or website owner) to pass out. You want your audience to be able to bring home more than just new poultry knowledge. You'll also gain a reputation as someone that is knowledgeable about poultry and that could open new avenues for selling your items.

Create a Workshop

Step 1: Define the Goals

You need to have a goal for your workshop. What is it that you want to pass on to people in your presentation? It could be to provide information on basic chicken care, how to incubate eggs and raise chicks, showing your chicken or many other topics.

Step 2: Decide Who Would like to Attend (who is your audience)

Are you in a rural area or the country? City? Where you are will dictate who comes to your workshop. If you're in the city part of your workshop could be on keeping city chickens. If you're in the country, it could be on best laying breeds for the country. Beyond that the attendees will be of varying ages and genders. That's one bonus to having your topic as chickens- it covers a wide range of possible attendees.

Step 3: Choose the Right Location

If you have ten attendees, then the feed store backroom or warehouse will probably be just fine. But if you have 50 people, you may have to find an outside location that's large enough.

You also need to have enough parking if you expect a large crowd. If you set up sign-up sheets beforehand, you can get a good idea of how many will be attending and be able to make changes as needed.

Step 4: Create an Agenda

Anticipating what questions your attendees may have in their minds is important. You want to be able to answer their questions. That's why they would come to your workshop.

To set up an interesting presentation:

- **Main points** – Decide on your main topic. Break down the topic into smaller segments for easier understanding. If your topic is chicken care, break it down into housing, feeding and egg laying for example.
- **Visual aids** – Even if your topic is interesting people like to see some visual aids. Using a projector, or some video keeps things interesting. You can also use live props for demonstration such as a live chicken, different size eggs, nail clippers, for instance.
- **Discussions and activities** –always leave time for discussion. Activities keep things interesting. For small children, you can offer pictures of chickens and farm activities. For adults, you can schedule in activities such as: how to trim nails, check for external parasites, or how to tell one type of feed from another.

Step 5: Develop a Follow-up Plan

At the end of your workshop have a questionnaire ready. Ask for their opinions of your talk and how well they liked or disliked it. The feedback will help you to refine your workshop for future events.

During the Workshop – Getting People Involved

One thing that makes a workshop fun is getting to be involved rather than just listen to a lecture. If you plan on making your topic about basic chicken care you can invite people to bring their chickens so they can learn to trim nails. If you have your own chickens you'd like to bring to trim, you could do that as one example.

Another example is to bring different types of feed and after talking about it, allow the audience to try their hand at pointing out the different types. Encourage everyone to become involved.

Some Workshop Tips

Here are a few more ideas for running a successful workshop:

- To get everyone relaxed and comfortable start the workshop with a few icebreakers.
- Sometimes, not everyone has to stay for the entire workshop. Have your handouts set aside so that people that have to leave early can pick up your handouts on the way out.
- Many people work during the day so hold your workshop in the evening or on the weekends. Your group will probably be more energetic if you schedule the event in the morning or late afternoon. (If you have to run the workshop in the early afternoon, make sure there's plenty of strong coffee available!)

Key Points

Planning a workshop isn't easy but the more you put into it, the more enjoyable it will be for your audience. You want your audience to leave your workshop happy that they attended.

The goals of the workshop should be at the center of all your planning. Fun visual aids and activities will keep everyone relaxed and involved. Don't forget to follow up afterward: Although it can be scary to hear what people really thought of all your hard work, it's the only way you'll improve your future events.

Chapter 6: Selling chicks/ducklings, young and adult birds

Button Quail chicks

Buy/sell chickens of all ages

If you like dealing with people, buying and selling and raising birds you can be a chicken, duck and/or quail dealer. This is a person who has different kinds of the chosen poultry of different ages that he sells from chicks and ducklings up to mature roosters and drakes.

You can keep pairs and hatch your own eggs. You could sell those eggs. You could incubate and hatch the eggs and sell the chicks or ducklings. If you hold onto the pullets, you could sell the pullets at the ready-to-lay age of five months for a higher price than a chick.

You could go to swaps and sales and buy chicks or ducklings to raise to resell as ready-to-lay or mature birds in singles, pairs or trios or even small flocks. You can frequent the livestock auctions and buy and sell your birds. (Remember to use quarantine procedures when introducing new birds).

If you don't have any restrictions, you can be the local person that people bring their unwanted chickens to and sell them. Many people can't or don't want roosters, so they are looking for someone to take them. Many people are happy to give you a rooster no matter what your plans are for him (eating, reselling or keeping).

Your best bet is to deal with all different breeds. How many different will depend on your resources. Having different breeds makes your opportunities to buy and sell greater than specializing in one breed.

Hatch eggs to sell chicks/ducklings (off the heat lamp)

Many people would love to have chicks and ducklings but don't want to deal with the heat lamp. For the first six weeks, or until feathered, the babies need to have a heat source if you do not have a hen or duck to hatch the eggs. With artificial incubation, once they hatch, they need a heat source. You can hatch the babies out and raise them until they are ready to go to new owners and go right into a coop.

Chicks and ducklings off the lamp typically cost a little more than a just-hatched baby. You need to factor in the upkeep costs for the six weeks and see what extra it cost to raise them to that age and factor the extra cost into the price of the babies.

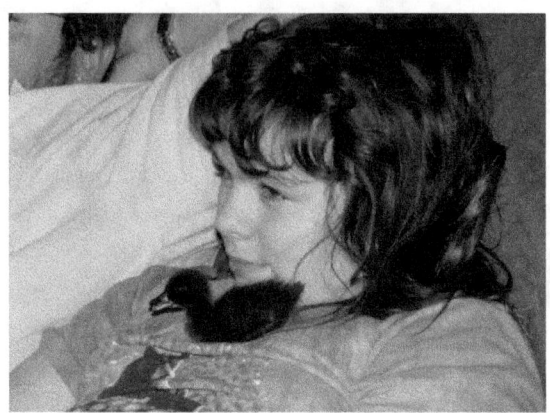

Melyssa Cappuccio with her hatchery East Indie duckling

Own a hatchery

Owning a hatchery would mean that you supply poultry (mostly chicks and ducklings), eggs or supplies to the public. There are two ways to run a hatchery- incubate the eggs yourself and sell them to the public or have people that work for you to incubate the eggs to provide you with chicks and ducklings to sell to the public.

If you want to incubate the eggs yourself you'll need incubators (the large cabinet type) and a large area to keep the incubators with electricity as well as have a brooding area for when the chicks and ducklings hatch. You'll need a place to box up them and be near enough to a post office that can handle your baby poultry for shipping. Keep in mind that one-day-old chicks and ducklings can be shipped and sent by two-day delivery but you wouldn't want it to take longer than that or to ship babies older than a day. Chicks and ducklings live on their yolk sack for a few days after hatching. It's too stressful to ship them once they have used up their yolk sack. Older birds can be offered for sale. A chick or duckling over a day or two old should not be shipped before it is three months old. Once the day old's shipping window of a day or two closes you'll do best for the chicks to wait until they are old enough to ship at a few months old.

All hatcheries use the United States Post Office for shipping chicks and ducklings. They require a special type of approved box with labels on the box. The post office does a good job of shipping them and has been doing it this way, with success, for many years.

You should also have a website, direct phone line and an email address. You are essentially setting up a business venture. Once you have your website, phone, email, location and equipment you are ready to start your business.

You will have to decide what breeds of chicks and ducklings you want to offer. The most successful hatcheries offer a variety of breeds, both standard and bantam sized. Many also offer eggs for the buyer to hatch chickens, ducks, game birds and supplies.

If you decide to let others incubate and hatch the chicks and supply them to you to fill orders you still would do well to have a website, printer, phone, and email as well as a steady list of suppliers. The breeds you offer will depend on what breeds your suppliers are hatching. You may be able to work out a contract that specifies your choice of what the supplier will incubate depending on some market research as to what breeds are most popular.

Sanitation and safety will be of utmost importance. Disease could easily wipe out your business, so it's important to make sure you are following state guidelines as well as rules and regulations for poultry operations.

Check with your state government agencies to find out what the protocols are for your business.

To set up a business takes an investment from you. Depending on whether you decide to incubate the eggs yourself or get chicks and ducklings from suppliers will account for how much of a monetary investment you need to make up front.

You'll need to advertise in as many places as you can. You can advertise in magazines, newspapers, online on your website, social media and sites devoted to chickens. You'll keep a database of your customers and their information. Make sure you have an attractive price list typed up to put online and to send to those who request it.

Keeping it local- if you plan just to supply the local population of customers you can keep your operation on the smaller scale compared to the big name hatcheries that ship all over. Selling local allows you to skip the shipping and offer direct pickup. Do some research beforehand to see if your hatchery will be viable in your area. If you live in the city that doesn't allow chickens, for example, your hatchery probably won't work out. If you live in a farming community or rural community that does allow chickens you may have enough of a customer base locally to keep your business going.

You'll need to find a supplier of your eggs if you are going to incubate the eggs yourself. You'll want a seller who adheres to local and state laws for poultry farming and keeps a clean, well-organized operation.

You'll need to have someone that knows how to work the financial part of your operations. Not only in billing the customer but paying suppliers, paying anyone working for you and keeping all buying and selling in order.

Whether a small local hatchery or a large operation that ships all over, you will want to do your research first. Check to see how other hatcheries operate. Talk to as many as you can to get some insight as to what is involved. Work with an accountant on the financial aspect of your business. The potential to make money in this market has many variables that you will have to research to tell whether your hatchery would be a viable business venture.

Russian Orloff chick

Raising chicks for resale to hatcheries

Some hatcheries rely on suppliers to provide chicks. Having suppliers is common with small or just starting out hatcheries. A hatchery may only incubate and hatch a few breeds themselves and need suppliers for other breeds.

You may be able to supply some rare breeds if you have a local hatchery or live near a hatchery. You could work with the hatchery to find out what breeds the hatchery has been getting requests for that they do not currently carry, or the hatchery may need additional suppliers for popular breeds.

If you can make a working relationship with your local hatcheries to provide healthy day olds you could have seasonal income with your day-olds. You can also supply eggs for hatching special breeds or if the hatchery has orders they cannot fill and look to you to help supply them. This is what is considered drop-shipping when you place an order with the company, and they arrange to have your items shipped directly from the supplier.

Sell point-of-lay pullets

Point-of-lay pullets are female chickens that are soon to start laying eggs. Typically they are around 5-6 months old. Point-of-lay (aka ready-to-lay) pullets can bring a good price and lots of people want them in all breeds, but mostly in the laying breeds like Rhode Island Red. Buying pullets at this time allows the chicken owner to be able to put the hen right into the coop (with an introduction period) and look forward to getting eggs in a short amount of time.

You can raise chicks for 5-6 months and ask a premium price. Check into what breeds are popular in your area and raise that breed and plan to have the pullets ready to go to new homes in spring when buyers are most actively looking for point-of-lay pullets.

Keep in mind the extra cost to raise a pullet to this age and price your pullets accordingly. You can check into what other people are charging for them in your area to give you an idea of how to price your pullets.

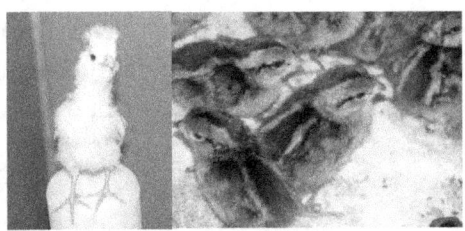

A Polish chicken chick and Bobwhite Quail chicks

Sell specific breeds

To sell a specific breed is known as a niche market. You are selling your breed to a smaller group of people that want that specific breed.

Once you have your selected breed, you need to get the word out that you have them available. Use social media as well as newspapers, magazines and club newsletters. At shows, you can set up a small display next to your cages to spotlight your selected breed.

To make your selected breed stand out, highlight what makes them different than other breeds. If you chose an Ameracauna, you could highlight that they lay blue eggs. Many people like something that is a little different and a blue egg certainly stands out. If you choose Silkies, you could highlight both the fur-like feathers they have as well as the temperament that makes them great for a family pet.

No matter what breed you choose, the key is to make the potential buyers aware of why you choose your breed over others and what it could do for them. It could be laying ability, size, egg color, brooding instincts or certain desired traits.

Many breeds have clubs where others who also like your chosen breed get together. It could be in person, or it could be online. Many breeds have groups on Facebook and social media websites like Backyardchickens.com. You can also make a webpage for your specific breed. On that page, you can show pictures as well as information about your chosen breed. If you sell hatching eggs, you can have them pay right off of your web page or direct them to contact you through email, text or phone.

Clubs often have shows and if you have a specific breed you have the opportunity to show them. A lot of shows also have a sales area. If you have your special breed for a while, people will remember that you have that breed and will seek you out. Other chicken people will refer potential buyers to you if they don't have your specific breed.

Selling day olds

If you do not want to invest in an incubator and deal with the hatching of eggs you can sell day olds. Ordering day olds would mean ordering day-old chicks from a hatchery and when they arrive two days after ship date you put them in a brooder and advertise them for sale. Chicks that have just hatched will live off of their egg yolk for two to three days after hatching. This gives hatcheries time to ship the newly hatched right to you without having to worry about the chicks not having food or water as they won't need it yet.

Selecting a hatchery is important. You want one that is as close as possible (being able to pick them up would be even better!), has a good reputation and offers your chosen breeds as the least expensive price. When pricing out your chicks remember to add in shipping to your calculations of how much it will cost per chick. If you have a good market in your area, you should be able to sell your chicks quickly. When calculating cost-per-chick account for the electricity for the heat lamp for at least two weeks, food, and any medicines/vitamins/supplements, you plan to give them. When you go to sell your chicks, you should ask at least double what your investment in the chick comes out to be when you sell them.

Chapter 7: Online Selling

A page from the Author's Website

Online selling - websites/blogs/email lists

Selling online is a must today to be able to offer your poultry to the widest audience possible. You can have a website built or do it yourself, or you can write a blog and make it profitable. You can also list your birds on sale sites like Craigslist, in the sale section on social sites like Backyardchickens.com or Facebook groups that allow sales postings.

Websites

Web sites can be simple do-it-yourself affairs for very little cost, or you can have an elaborate website for your farm featuring all your farm has to offer. Using your preferred search engine type in "free websites". Consider the top 3 on the list. Do some research as to what they have to offer. Often, in exchange for the free websites you have to allow advertising on your site. Look at other sites that are hosted by particular web hosts to see what kind of format they have and what the advertising looks like. Generally it will take a minimum of two or three days to set up a simple 2-3 page website. The web hosts have made it easier with step by step instructions on how to put together your own website.

As the other option, you can have a website made for you. You will give the web developer pictures and information, and they will put it together for you. Prices vary as it can cost a few hundred dollars to thousands depending on how elaborate it is.

If you are a member of a club, group or social network, ask what other people recommend. Very often you'll get to see examples of the many designs that are available- both do-it-yourself and custom made. The custom made ones typically will have a monthly or yearly fee to maintain your website and the web developer will charge you a small fee each time you want to update your website.

Whichever way you decide to set up your website, you will want to have a page for your poultry for sale. If you have different types of poultry, you might have different pages for each type or if you only have one type (say just chickens) you can have one sale page. Make sure that it only takes one click or two clicks from your homepage to get to your sales page, so people don't get lost trying to navigate your site. Keep your sales pages up to date. Include information such as breed, age, gender, and price.

Blogs

Blogs are a fun way to keep people informed about what is happening on your farm. There are free blog sites where you can set up your blog. A blog is a journal of the happenings in your life or on the farm.

You would log onto your blog on a regular basis, say weekly, and make a post about what when on in the previous week. If you had some chicks hatch that were for sale, you would list that along with the information that a buyer would want such as breed, gender, and price. People like to read about the more personal parts of a person's life. A cute story of how mama hen showed her chicks how to dust bath or a post talking about how a new family added six new chicks to the family. You'll get more followers if you keep the audience coming back again and again to read your blog posts.

On many blogs, you can advertise for other people. For instance, you can put ads up for a feed store that carries chicken supplies or an advertiser that sells coops. That is called online marketing. You get a small percentage of the sales for advertising their product on your site.

The main point of a blog is to make posts that keep people coming back to read each of your posts. Keep things fun and interesting and you may get a following of just a few people or hundreds of people- it's all up to you and the readers.

Email lists

Besides texting, email is one of the top ways people communicate electronically. Blogs and websites often have a button where you can be added to an email list to get notified by email when a new blog post has been put up or a website updated. If you have a lot of inquiries about your birds or products you can offer to put people on your email list so they can be notified when birds and such come up for sale. This works especially well if you are hatching chicks and can notify people when the chicks have hatched and are ready to go to new homes.

Keep in mind that for any lists you are putting together you want to assure people that the list is only to keep them updated on your farm and that it will not be sold. Having a person's email sold ends up with the owner of the email receiving lots of unwanted spam. Knowing you will only use their email for your list makes them more likely to accept your invitation to be on the list and potentially become a future buyer.

Email lists can be set up through your local email provider. Most email providers have a section available in your email program for groups. As each request comes in you add their email to the group list. When you have some news or something to sell you, send a mass email out to your group.

Most websites have an option to add an "add me to this group" button where a reader only has to click on the button to be added to a group list. If you get requests from different sources, you can manually put together your list through your email program.

More online selling

Social groups (Facebook). Facebook has a section called "groups" where like-minded people gather online. Most of these groups allow selling and, in fact, have a special section where you can post an ad.

Social websites- For almost everything you can think of there is a website out there devoted to it. Different types of animal sites are quite popular. A chicken website, for example, will have sections on breed types, chick color IDs, coop idea a breeder's listing section and a social area called a forum where questions are asked. Part of that forum will be a place to post about your chicken and show pictures. A popular part of such a site is the sale section usually divided into hatching eggs, chicks and adults as well as a section for game birds, waterfowl and other types of birds.

Chapter 8: More Selling Ideas

Have a "Down on the Farm" themed party
Display by Jeckaroonie Balloons, LLC

Birthday parties

Birthday parties featuring animals are very popular. Pony rides are a particular favorite. To make money, you can offer a "farm" like experience by bringing some calm chickens, ducks and/or quail to visit a birthday party. The birds should be used to being held and petted. Their nails should be trimmed, and they should have a bath the day before, so they are clean and smell nice. Some people I have seen put a chicken harness on the chicken with a leash to keep hold of the chicken. This is a small harness much like a dog would wear.

To set up your place for the children to meet the birds could be something like this: bring two bales of hay. You can have a nice miniaturized picket fence set up behind the bales with a sign that reads something catchy and cute such as, "We are EGGsited it is your Birthday!" You can sit on the bale, and with a small towel in your lap, hold a chicken, duck or quail for the children to pat. You can have your other birds you bring along set nearby so the kids can see them. You can tell a little story about the particular bird or birds, in general, or a combination of the two. You can invite the children up to pet the bird. You can offer photo opportunities by letting the children hold a docile bird in their laps. As part of your presentation, you can have a helper take photos of each child to take home with them. You could do such things as: reading a book featuring a chicken, duck or quail or have a drawing of a bird for the children to take home. You could also offer a "goody" bag to each child with things such as a chicken sticker, drawing of a duck with 2-3 crayons, a candy or other treat, an eraser shaped like an egg, a picture of a chicken etc.

The amount to charge varies on what you provide. You can keep it simple and just bring your chicken, a couple of chairs and a towel and let the kids pat the chicken. Or you can go all out with a story, pictures, goody bags and a chance to hold a chicken, duck or quail. It's all up to what your willing to put together, and the amount of time you want to make each visit. Generally a parent would like a half an hour "show".

This kind of thing is often shared by word of mouth. Many parents share what went on at their child's birthday party. A poultry show at a party is unconventional but connecting it to the idea of "farm" helps to spread the word about your presentation. You can put ads up locally online or in your local papers. Make up a business card to post and pass around and talk up your show. If you make a good presentation, geared toward children, you can become a popular local celebrity and make some nice green for your pocket.

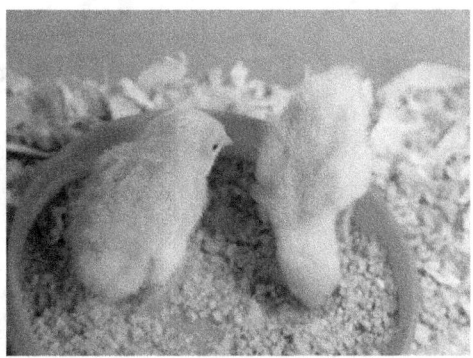

Two chicks in a classroom setting

Classroom experience

Many classrooms today are allowing the students the joys of hatching eggs. Most children love the experience of seeing the little balls of fluff being hatched. A profit can be made in putting together a package for the classrooms to rent to hatch eggs. This will consist of the incubator, instruction on how to hatch the eggs, or a booklet you've put together, and the fertile eggs themselves. Many classrooms would not know what to do with the chicks once hatched so you could offer to take any chicks back that the kids (or rather a kid's parents would agree to) would take home.

Make up a written contract spelling out what services and items you will provide. Also, list what the responsibility and fees of the teacher would be. Spell out if you'll replace the eggs to try again if the first eggs don't hatch. Once the contract is signed and you have mutually decided on a date for delivery you can bring your incubator, thermometer and a hygrometer, and fresh fertile eggs. If the teacher will be keeping the new hatchlings any length of time they will also need a brooder, shavings, paper towels (to go over the shavings for the first couple of days), water dish with marbles, food dish and chick food. Keep in mind you'll need an incubator that you can see the eggs. Some cheaper models are almost totally enclosed and make it difficult to see the chicks. The whole point is to be able to watch the process so being able to see the eggs is important.

If you are taking the chicks back with you, you will be able to sell those chicks either right away or raise them to a certain age and sell them for additional profit.

As part of your package, you could also do a presentation to the class. You could describe the process and what they can expect to happen, and if all goes well, the result will be some happy, healthy chicks.

Future Farmers of America and 4-H.

These community conscious groups for kids have been around 1928 for FFA and 1902 for 4-H.

Future Farmers of America was founded to a greater opportunity for self-expression and the development of leadership. In this way they will develop confidence in their ability and have pride in working as a farmer to, "help young people learn about farm life and 4-H was founded help young people and their families gain the skills needed to be proactive forces in their communities' and develop ideas for a more innovative economy". These days there are just as many girls as boys in this group.

4-H opened the door for young people to learn leadership skills and revolutionized how youth connected to practical, hands-on learning experiences outside the classroom. 4-H has a variety of projects with many being with animals.

For both groups, clubs are available that feature chickens and other poultry, teach children about how to care for their animals. They also learn what is involved in daily care with shows and fairs available to show their birds and eggs. The kids raise the poultry and on fair day they show their bird and offer them for sale that the new owner can pick up at the end of the fair.

You can incubate and hatch eggs for projects for the kids in these groups. You can sell them chicks, or you can raise the chicks until laying age and make the young hens available to kids as projects. Some clubs may put together an incubator and brooder, and you can sell fertile eggs for them to hatch.

Bgforhunting by Hester, Dr. F. Eugene

Hunting (Quail & Duck hunts and offering your property for hunting for a fee)

Quail hunting is a popular sport. Some people use dogs to help flush the quail and retrieve the birds. Many types of quail are hunted for sport. When training dogs for hunting, pen raised quail are often used (See training bird dogs). Quail can only be hunted at certain times of the year and varies with the type of method used a rifle, bow, or falcons.

If you own a large tract of land, you can offer hunters a place to hunt on your property for a fee. You can also host quail hunts. You would need to make sure you have enough quail on your property for these ventures. You can couple it with raising quail to restock and also offer the quail to other land owners to stock their properties. Permits are required to hunt and release birds so check with your state Department of Fish and Game for any special regulations and permits needed.

Quail hunting is popular, particularly in the south where the quail of choice is the Northern Bobwhite Quail. If you want to run quail hunts on your property as a way to make some money from quail, there are some things that you will need to supply. First is a suitable habitat for the quail.

Quail do best in a habitat that has open fields, broken grounds with crops or burned and allowed to grow native plants, a water source, and low brush. The fields and crop grounds provide food in the forms of seeds and bugs. They like brushy areas with patches of woods that offer places to escape predators, rest, and nest. They also need roosting fields of knee-high vegetation nearby. If any of this is missing on your property, it will have few, if any, quail.

If you are to be an all-inclusive hunting preserve for hunting quail, you will need vehicles to get the hunters place to place, guides who are familiar with hunting quail and bird hunting dogs. You should be able to provide hunters with your dogs or allow them to bring their own.

As an bonus to the hunters, if you can offer to dress the birds they have hunted that will be another plus in what you have to offer a hunter.

Lease out your property to farmer

This option will enable you to take in some extra money if you have land you are not using.

If you have land that is not in use, or you would like to offer it to others to use you could consider leasing out your land. Many farmers will pay a fee to be able to graze animals on leased land or hay it for feed. Check the current value of leased land to see what kind of lease fee you could charge to let others make use of your land.

Make sure you have a contract, and it spells out exactly what can be done with the property, so there are no misunderstandings down the road. If they wanted to graze cows and thought, they would like also to have a flock of chickens in the future, make sure that your contract states exactly how the land can be used.

Some locations may require you to have insurance on the land so make sure you check into local rules on land use and insurance if you are leasing out the land.

Make chicken diapers

Yes, chicken diapers are a real thing. For people that are keeping a chicken in the house either as a pet or because it is ill, a chicken diaper is a way to keep the chicken poop under control. There are different types of chicken diapers but most typically go around the bird's body to hold a small scoop over the vent to catch all the chicken poop. Velcro or small plastic snaps can be used. They are typically adjustable for a good fit. They come in all sizes.

You can set up an Etsy or Ebay store and sell chicken diapers if you have a sewing machine. Chicken owners like to have a choice of patterns and colors. If you are interested in making chicken diapers you could order a few examples from people that already have stores set up or are selling them online. Make some examples and take pictures of them on your chickens. Advertise on social media, at swap meets and magazines. Give a few away to get reviews that you could post on a web page, social media or an online store.

A chicken saddle – Photo by Amanda LaMantia

Make chicken saddles

You're probably wondering what a chicken saddle is. Basically, it's a covering for hens when roosters are getting too aggressive with or they also work well to help shield healing wounds on the back.

Roosters have spurs on their legs and when they mate with the hens sometimes all the activity breaks off or pulls out the hen's back and side feathers. Chicken saddles offer protection to the hen from the rooster. The rooster can still mate with the hen, and the hen has protection from the spurs.

As with the chicken diapers, you can make these if you have a sewing machine. Invest in buying a few examples and do research on the types that are available. Come up with your own design or model after the examples you purchased and make your own to sell to others. You can sell them online in one of the online stores like Etsy or one of the popular auction sites. If you like sewing you could also make chicken diapers and sell both.

Frank and Melyssa Cappuccio with movie chicken "Sticky"- a bantam Cochin

Movies

Poultry, chickens, in particular, are seen in the movies, tv shows and commercials often. If you have a particular chicken or duck, you think would be great in these areas you could consider having them as an actor.

Check online (such as www.backstage.com or www.Actorsequity.com) noting when it will need actors or extras for upcoming movies. You can find proper representation by looking in film directories or calling film companies for reputable agencies that deal with animal actors.

 You will need to be able to "sell" your chicken or duck to the production company. An agency will be able to offer the company photos and a resume on your chicken or duck. It would be helpful if your bird is tolerant of bright lights, loud noises and lots of hustle and bustle. You can train your bird, using a clicker, to do basic commands such as to look up, walk from one spot to another or peck at an object. Have your bird's talent on their resume.

Some tips:

The more "tricks" your bird can do, the more desireable they will be.

Talk to other people who supply animals for movies and TV. Even if they are a dog trainer and not a chicken trainer, a lot of the same methods will also apply to your birds.

When checking out talent agencies ask for a resume or work history. You may have to pay a fee up front, but it should not exceed $50. Any more than that is a warning sign. Most pet agencies are happy to take you on their books and take a percentage of the earnings rather than charge you up front.

Be prepared- it's not all glamor. Days can be very long and sometimes take all night with a lot of waiting in between. Sometimes a handler/trainer is hired to oversee the work the animals on the set will be doing. All you would be asked to do would be to drop off your animal and pick them up at the end of day. With an exotic type animal, like a chicken, you may be the only one who knows how to handle them. You probably would be needed on the set to direct your chicken to do what the director is asking.

Working on set can be a long, boring and tiring experience but to work through to the end and see your pet on the screen is one that you don't forget.

Offer "kits" of henhouse, coop, hens or chicks (rent or sell)

Another idea to make money is to offer a "package" or "kit" and either sell or rent this "package" out. What you would offer is a small coop/henhouse, hens, water and feed dishes and feed. The customer would pay one price for this package, and the number of hens can vary and be priced accordingly. This would work particularly well for residential or backyard families that just want to have some fresh eggs.

You would want the coop/henhouse to comfortably fit the number of hens. For a large number of hens, you would want a coop you could take down and move if you are doing a rental situation. Ideally you would want small groups like 3, 4 or 6 hens. Larger amounts of hens might not be practical because the size of the coop would have to be larger, but it could be done.

You would want to have a contract with people that would rent your package. Say, for example, a four-person family wanted to rent four hens. You would bring them a henhouse/coop setup for four hens, water and feed dishes and a month worth of feed. They would handle the care of the hens, and they keep the eggs. If the agreed on rental were spring to fall, for example, you could supply the feed as needed and in the fall pick up the coop/henhouse and the hens for the winter and rent the package out again in the spring.

As an alternative, you can offer a package for sale rather than rent. You would supply the same things as in a rent situation but they would be buying the package, and it would be their responsibility after the purchase. This is a good option for first-time chicken owners who do not have anything set up for chickens.

Operating as a farm on your taxes

I thought I'd include this as many people wonder if they can operate as a business and get a refund if expenses outweigh the income.

The goal of a business is to make money. If you fail to make a profit, you can claim deductions on your taxes as a business to offset the money you put into the business. For example if you were to operate as a business you would claim expenses such as feed, medicines for the birds, vet bills, egg cartons if you sell eggs, etc.

Farmers may have different ways of creating income with the sale of livestock, produce, grains, and other products raised or bought for resale as the most common. The entire amount a farmer receives, including money and the fair market value of any property or services, are reported on IRS section of Profit or Loss From Farming.

Regulations vary state to state. Most have a rule of having to make a profit x amount of years out of x years in business. If you continually fail to make any profit, yet still continue to claim as a business. and get audited you may end up being declared a hobby rather than a business. They may require you to repay your tax refund for your business expenses back to the government that you received in previous years. Hopefully, you will make a profit and be a success in your farm venture. If you just keep having losses year after year you may want to consider not filing as a business and just keeping your small operation as a hobby. You can still make money that will go into your pocket, you just won't declare yourself as a business and be eligible for tax refunds on it. Rules may also apply that even as a hobby if you make over a certain amount you need to file as a business. Check with your local authority on what your rules are in your state.

The online IRS website states, "Among the deductible expenses are amounts paid to farm labor. If a farmer pays his child to do farm work and a true employer-employee relationship exists, reasonable wages or other compensation paid to the child is deductible. The wages are included in the child's income, and the child may have to file an income tax return. These wages may also be subject to social security and Medicare taxes if the child is age 18 or older."

Another deductible expense is depreciation. Farmers can depreciate most types of tangible property — except land — such as buildings, machinery, equipment, vehicles, certain livestock, and furniture. Farmers can also depreciate certain intangible property, such as copyrights, patents, and computer software. To be depreciable, the property must

- Be property the farmer owns
- Be used in the farmer's business or income-producing activity
- Have a determinable life
- Have a useful life that extends substantially beyond the year placed in service

Some expenses paid during the tax year may be partly personal and partly business. Examples include gasoline, oil, fuel, water, rent, electricity, telephone, automobile upkeep, repairs, insurance, interest, and taxes. Farmers must allocate these expenses between their business and personal parts. The personal part of these expenses is not deductible.

For example, a farmer paid $1,500 for electricity during the tax year. He used one-third of the electricity for personal purposes and two-thirds for farming. Under these circumstances, two-thirds of the electricity expense, or $1,000, is deductible as a farm business expense. Records must be maintained to document the business portion of the expense.

Information about other deductible expenses and reporting requirements can be found in IRS Publication 225, Farmer's Tax Guide."

If you want to operate as a business read the thorough booklet stated above and talk with your accountant and see if your operation would be considered a business or a hobby and how you would go about filing as a business and claiming deductions.

"Duckie" loves to cuddle

Pet therapy

Most pet therapy is a volunteer operation, but there are opportunities you can offer such as trainer of a therapy animal. Pet therapy can be done with domestic animals including chickens, ducks, and quail.

There are many groups to be found online that offer therapy animals. Joining is typically free and some offer classes for modest amounts. This is where you can join with other people who have such interest and make some connections.

As a trainer of a pet therapy animal, you would want to select a pet that has a calm disposition and will sit or lay still while being petted or when they are beside or on a person. They cannot bite or scratch. Some therapy chickens benefit by wearing a chicken diaper to catch any droppings during a visit. Learning to wear this device does take some getting used to.

As a successful trainer, you can hold classes on how to have a pet become a therapy animal and charge a small fee. This would offer you the opportunity to hold a class or workshop in different communities. People could bring their pet to you and you can go over the basic requirements for a pet therapy animal. You could then work with each animal teach the owner to teach the pet basic commands such as stay and lay down.

Pet therapy is a very rewarding experience. People in hospitals or assisted living facilities and nursing homes often are delighted to have a certified therapy pet. The therapy animal can bring back memories of living on the farm for the older generation or just delight being able to touch and hold an unusual therapy pet, like a chicken.

You may not be paid for your services, but such training could add value to your pet. Any expenses you incur providing therapy, including mileage, uniform, and extra expenses for grooming, may be tax deductible.

The author with pet Serama chicken "Pepper"

Pets/companions/House Chickens

A chicken can be a wonderful pet and companion. The best pets are the ones that connect with you whether it be by enjoying a snack you bring them or being content to sit on your lap. Many people enjoy just sitting down and watching the chicken go about doing what chickens do- scratch, wander around, peck and other chicken behaviors.

Chicken watching can be quite relaxing. Even if you are up and about changing water, sweeping or doing any of the tasks that having chickens takes can be considered time well spent. Many people have a chair or bench in their coop just to be able to sit and enjoy the company of the chickens.

A chicken that has a pleasing personality is more likely to sell than one that does not particularly if the buyer is looking mainly for a pet. You could even get more money for a sweet tempered chicken that likes your attention than one that is standoffish.

Having a chicken as a house pet is not unheard of. The problem with a house chicken is that they poop whenever and wherever they feel the need to go. Some people use the sanitized wipe and just wipe and go as they occur, others keep the chicken in their lap on a special towel or even, and yes I am not kidding, diapers for chickens.

Smaller chickens are popular as house pets. The smaller the chicken, the more money you can sell it for. If you're very small chicken (like a Serama or Old English Game Bantam) is raised in a household environment, has a calm and friendly disposition, they will bring a better than average price.

"Pasha" Ameraucana hen

Photographer at shows

Animal photographers must have an eye for capturing clear and interesting images of their animal subjects. They must have knowledge of how to use flashes, various lenses, as well as other equipment need for weather and lighting conditions. It is helpful to have knowledge of animal behavior as well. At a chicken show or event, people are proud of their birds, and if you are a good photographer, people will pay to have a professional photograph taken.

While a traditional film camera used to be the norm, most animal photographers have made the switch to digital photography. As the photographer, it is up to you to decide which method to use. Ultimately, most film images are scanned and transferred to digital format so going digital may be saving you steps.

Specialized computer software is used by most photographers to crop and manipulate images, so technology and computer skills are generally of a high value. Having a professional online portfolio to showcase their work and advertise to potential clients is always a benefit and should be utilized.

You can specialize by photographing one specific category of animals such as wildlife, or individual species like chickens.

Contact show managers to make sure you are allowed to set up at the event. Once at the show or event you can set up your area. You can have a helper walk around the show or event passing out a flier showing that you are there and what you can do for a chicken owner. You could also put an ad in the club newsletter that is putting on the show. Once you get someone interested, even if it's just to check out what you are offering, you can show them samples and offer to take pictures of their chickens. If you are just starting out, you should price reasonably. Beforehand figure out how much each photo costs in terms of printing out the photo. Hopefully, you already have a suitable camera that takes quality photos.

At a show or event, your backdrop for taking the photos can be as simple as a plain one-color sheet or blanket over a cardboard support. You can make your support as you would a tri-fold display. It needs to be strong enough to hold your sheet, cloth or blanket without falling over. This can be done by using a heavy object, like a brick, to sit behind the tri-fold. Typically you'll have to custom make a setting for the backdrop.

Besides shows and events, some animal photographers focus on supplying images to stock photo agencies. The photographer earns a commission when the stock agency licenses a client to use the image for a fee. The photos can be for used in advertisements, magazines, books, or websites.

A degree in photography or photojournalism would be helpful but is not necessary. Even some single classes in photography would be helpful. The most helpful thing for aspiring photographers is to gain experience from those who are already an expert in the business. This could be taking classes or finding a mentor. Photography can be a very technical art, and there are items of equipment that must be mastered, not to mention having experience in knowing when and how to capture just the right moment to snap the shutter button.

Many communities have groups or clubs for anyone interested in photography. Aspiring photographers can connect with experienced professionals, as well as provide a forum for discussing new techniques and emerging technology in the field.

According to Yahoo answers, the best answer was that pet photography is a very limited field. There is a market, but it is a very small one. How much? The average photographer makes in the US $37,000 USD. It is estimated that a photographer specializing in pets would make about half that. That being said, if you live in a large urban or wealthy area, you may be able to make the same yearly salary as a general photographer.

A separate salary for a pet photographer is not listed on The Bureau of Labor Statistics (BLS) but the 2010 salary survey found that photographers earned a mean annual wage of $35,980 ($17.30 per hour). The lowest 10 percent earned less than $17,350 ($8.34 per hour) while the highest 10 percent earned more than $63,400 ($30.48 per hour).

The BLS survey results also showed that the top paying states for photographers by annual mean wage in May of 2011 were the District of Columbia ($56,110), New York ($48,630), Virginia ($43,390), Connecticut ($53,810) and Illinois ($45,220).

Being a freelance pet photographer can be a fun and rewarding career depending on your location and the population in your area. Check into local clubs and groups that may be interested in your services.

Muscovy Duck

Rescue

There are many chicken lovers who would not turn away a chicken needing a new home. Most rescue chickens are roosters, but there are also hens that need new homes. The same would hold true if you were interested in rescuing other species such as ducks and quail. There are very few rescues for farm animals, but they do exist. If you have a soft heart and want to rescue chickens you can get funds to care for those rescues by fundraising and donations. You would want to become a 501C not-for-profit organization so you would get tax breaks.

Even not-for-profit organizations have a group of people who are paid to run the organization. If you set up a rescue you could be one of those paid persons.

Not only will you be taking care of chickens but you'll need to invest time and resources into management, planning and fundraising. One person can care for some of the animals but if your rescue gets large, you may need to bring in additional people to help run the rescue.

Start out with a plan: where you are going to put the rescues, you'll need a place to quarantine new arrivals and have a hospital sick bird area. You'll need to have a place to store feeds and medicines.

Talk with anyone that you can that has anything to do with a rescue. Check out library books, talk with knowledgeable people, visit other operations, attend workshops and classes. You'll soon meet a lot of people that can be a network for your own rescue.

Make out a mission statement. Define your purpose (taking in chickens that need new homes). A mission statement also says how you will go about running your rescue such as how you plan to rehome any chickens that are suitable to be adopted out.

If you are going to run as a not-for-profit, you'll need a mission statement. If you apply for any grants, and when you do fundraising, mission statements are a must. Being a non-profit doesn't mean you can't pay the staff of the rescue to take care of the animals and run the organization.

Set goals for your rescue. Write down concrete statements about what you need to achieve in order to fulfill your mission. Focus on results and the actions needed to achieve them. Start with your long-range goals and work back to the present. Where do you want to be in 10 years? (The answer to this question will give you your long-range goals.) What will you need to do to get there? (intermediate goals) Lastly, decide which of these goals you'll work on in the first and second year. (These are your short-range goals; you'll want to focus on these right away). Your goals should be inspiring and motivational!

For tax purposes, you'll want to have a system that documents the income and expenses. An accountant or bookkeeper can help you with the paperwork. An accountant should be able to help you set up your rescue as a not-for-profit using the 501C program.

A Labor of Love
Starting an organization to rescue animals is labor intensive but also richly rewarding on many different levels. Every adoption represents a victory in lifesaving work. Every individual that you reach with your message of compassion and caring for the animals will share the message with others. New friends will be made at meetings and events. Your effort will not only help many, of the community's animals, but it will build a strong alliance of people who care about animals. The message you put out of the compassion for animals will start with one person, you, and grow like an old tree with many limbs branching out and reaching out to others to start everyone talking about the cause for compassion for animals. And that's what it's all about!

Ceramic or Glass Figurines are Popular

Sell chicken collectibles (or other poultry collectibles!)

It's a well-known fact that people who like chickens, like to have chicken collectibles. From chicken themed curtains for the kitchen to little crystal statues of a hen and her chicks, chicken collectibles are popular.

You can start your own small business selling chicken themed collectibles. Some popular collectibles are dishcloths, curtains, plates and dinnerware, clothing, nick-nacks, books, CDs, DVDs, homemade crafts, slippers to name just a handful. You can set up a website or sell your collectibles on sites like Etsy, Ebay or Amazon. You can also set up a website where people can buy direct from you. You can set up a display at pet and farm tradeshows, chicken shows and chicken events like swaps and sales.

You can start small and work from home and sell through the internet. Scour flea markets, yard sales and auctions for chicken themed items. Keep in mind when buying that you plan to resell so estimate how much you can resell something for before you spend money on buying it. Once you have some items to sell, you can go on Ebay and set up a "store" online and sell via the auctions. There are lots of sites where you can step-by-step build your own website.

Etsy is an online marketplace designed exclusively for people selling handmade and vintage items. You can sell a pretty wide range of items. The only thing you really can't do on Etsy is sell brand new items or any item made by someone else.

Sellers have online stores, just like you've seen on eBay. They photograph their items, list them on the site, and once an item sells, they ship it out. Shipping costs are always paid by the buyer.

Etsy has no membership fee and lets you list an item for just 20 cents for four months. Keep in mind they do charge a 3.5% fee of the sale price of your item. They boast of a community of 30 million buyers and creative businesses.

Ebay is the one of the best place to sell online and make money. With over 100 million buyers, eBay is one of the world's largest online marketplaces. Using a step by step template you list your item with photos and description as well as a price. You can list a "buy it now" price if you know the market value of your item, or you can set a starting price and have it sell at an auction. Your first 20 items have no insertion fees. Ebay makes most of their profit on the fees they collect if you sell an item that can range from 4% to 10%. If you sell more than the twenty, you might consider opening an Ebay store.

Amazon has over 95 million monthly unique visitors. You have two options when selling on Amazon: to sell as an individual and to sell as a professional. If you plan on selling more than 40 items, you may consider selling as a professional. The difference is in the fee structure- how much it is to list your item and the amount they collect once you sell your item. Amazon has over 95 million monthly unique visitors. As an individual seller, Amazon charges you 15% Selling commission plus 99¢ per sale. The fee to become a professional seller is $39.95 per month, but as a pro seller you are only charged 15% --and not the extra 99¢. So if you sell 40 items per month or more, you will actually save money on fees. FBA- stands for Fulfillment By Amazon. This is an option where you send your items into Amazon, and they handle all the customer service and sales. The fees are higher with this option but if you are selling many items a day it saves you having to send out those items yourself as Amazon will take care of that for you.

You can also set up a simple display of a portable table with a nice tablecloth with a selection of some of your unique items. You can use a tri-fold cardboard with information about your business, pictures of some of your items and where to contact you and find your items. Making fliers for potential customers to take as well as some business cards will help pass the word. You can bring your set-up to chicken shows, sales and events where people interested in chickens will be.

You can also list your items in the sales sections of social media websites as well as other social media sites like Facebook. Check your group's rules before listing anything for sale as some may not allow selling or have a sister group just for selling.

If you enjoy going to estate auctions, yard sales and the like and also enjoy selling fun items like chicken memorabilia, selling chicken themed collectible may be a fun way for you to do what is fun and exciting and make money doing it.

Home Composting – Sell For Gardens

Sell manure

Why not make some money selling a by-product from your chickens and quail? Everyone that has these birds will have manure. A very successful business was made by one farmer who had cows and horses. She packaged the dry manure and offered it as a "soil conditioner" for plants. She packaged them like teabags, and you soak it in water to make a tea that you put on the soil around your plants to help them grow better. She now has a website and since starting her business in 2005, it has grown 30% a year. Her suggested price is three for $12.95 or 9 for $21.95. The bags are 3" x 5" (made larger, so they are not confused with human tea bags) She sells it over the internet using her website and sells directly to customers all over the world. Why not try that with chicken manure?

Another option is to collect your chicken manure into a compost bin or pile. Keep it free of trash and weeds. Turn it every couple of months and have it in a place where it can drain properly and be dried by the sun and wind. After eight months, your compost should be ready to sell. You can offer it by the bucket load, bag or truckload depending on how much you have to sell and your customer's preference. You can advertise in local papers and bulletin boards for pickup at your location, or you can contact landscapers in your area. Landscapers are picky and may require you to deliver it to them or have a certain amount that they can get from you. They also require it be clean and debris free.

One popular way to sell your manure is this method:

Create three large compost areas (for a small facility go with one pile). Put only manure in the pile with minimal wood fiber like shavings.

Hose down the piles regularly to help the decomposition process. Once a week turn the pile over.

After three months bag the manure. Using a 50 lb grain bag would work well. Sell it directly from your location to local people, local feed and farm stores, nurseries and landscapers.

Keep a list of your customers and when you are getting ready to have some compost available, let your list know so they will know when it is available.

You can "brand" your manure by making tags that go on every bag, so people know where to go to get more. You could bring some empty bags with the tags on them to farmer's markets so residents could pre-buy the bag and come out to your location when it fits into their schedule and pick up the compost.

Depending on how much manure your chickens produce you could allow other people to bring their manure to you, and you can compost it.

If you have a resource like manure, why not have it make some money for you? It can help offset the expense of having your chickens at the very least.

Various poultry supplies

Sell supplies

Selling chicken supplies could be a fun way to make some money, and it is chicken related. You will need to find suppliers for the items you want to sell. You'll want to save money on your purchases where you are, so take into consideration the supplier's price, if shipping is free and if there are discounts for multiple purchases. You'll want to find a wholesaler. This is a person who gets the items from a manufacturer and sells to suppliers like you. You will be marking up the items when you sell them. You'll need an outlet to sell your supplies. You can set up a booth and go to fairs, shows, and swaps, or you can sell online- see Selling Chicken Collectibles for information on Etsy, Ebay and Amazon selling.

Travelling Zoo

A traveling zoo is where you have a trailer set up where you can bring a handful of animals to various locations for fairs, birthday parties, and many various events. People looking to add some entertainment for the smaller kids would love to have you come to their even with a half dozen animals that can be petted and held and will pay for it. If you have just chickens, you can bring four to six of your tamest hens or young birds. It would be wise to have a helper along so you can work with two children at a time- particularly at an event the public will be passing through. For Birthday parties or some smaller events, like a library story time or giving a small talk on chickens, you could have one or two chickens for people to look at.

Typically you'll need two chairs for you and your helper to sit on. Two towels to drape over your or the kids laps and for an exhibit you would want a tri-fold board with pictures and easy to read basic information. Your cages that you will be using should be clean, neat and in good repair with fresh bedding in them. Remember to bring water and food for them as well.

You can advertise in local town papers, online town sites and putting up a business card wherever it is allowed like grocery stores and coffee shops. Use online resources like Craigslist and groups that are local.

Write how-to books

If you like to write (or these days- type) and enjoy gathering information, writing how-to books could be for you. How-to books come in all shapes, sizes and subjects. If you enjoy chickens, and you have the knowledge about their care, you can write a how-to book. These days there are online publishers that will publish your book for you. They have a site where they have a step by step instructions on how to publish your work.

Even if you don't know a great deal about a subject, if you can gather all the information from other sources. You then can write on any subject and add your gathered information to your well of knowledge. This requires a lot of reading and research. You'll need to be able to organize your thoughts and put them to paper and merge all your gathered information into something that offers a reader something interesting and new to read.

How to start writing a book:

Prepare yourself to spend a LOT of time writing and researching. Writing a book takes a lot of time. Stay focused and try to keep your time on your book.

Set aside some designated time for you to work on your book every day. This helps you get into the mindset of writing and makes concentration easier.

Start by making a skeleton. The skeleton is the basic idea of your book. This is especially important when writing a how-to book. After you have a list of the topics your book will cover, break that down into smaller sections (chapters). Make notes in each chapter of what that chapter will cover.

Do your research. Read all you can find and make notes on your different topics your book will cover. Once you have done as much research as you can for your topic, organize it in a way that you can refer to it once you begin the actual writing of the book. You may still be doing some research as you go as you may want further information or need something clarified.

Start small- plan on 300 words a day. This is approximately a page. How long it takes depends on you and how long it takes you to write or type and how much of your story or information you have to gather together.

When you are finished look for someone to edit for you. They should be someone who knows how to edit books. Get some opinions on your book once edited. This will help your book succeed. No one wants to read a poorly written book no matter what the topic.

When your book is done, you can find a publisher or you can self-publish. There are some wonderful publishing companies that has a do-it-yourself programs online that you can use to get your book published. Amazon has its own publishing company that will list your ebooks but also help you to get your book in print through Createspace. Createspace is a print-on-demand publisher that will print and send your books when you get orders for them.

If you like doing research, organizing information and like typing you will enjoy writing a book. The way you make money is through royalties. Each time your book sells the publisher gets a portion, and you get a portion. This is typically accrued monthly, and you can get a check or have it direct deposited.

Chapter 9: More Ideas Specific to Quail

A Tuxedo Northern Range Coturnix hen

Dog training (selling wings and use of live bird)

Many dog trainers use a quail's wing to train their hunting dogs. Chukar and Bob-Whites are common types of quail used in dog training. The best type of quail to sell to a dog trainer are quail raised in as natural an environment as possible that mimics a natural environment. This would involve having brush and similar cover for the birds and having as little contact with people as possible, so they act as wild as possible in a pen raised situation. When they are six weeks old, they go into flight pens that are made up of a similar environment as is naturally found in the area and large enough for them to build up their flight muscles.

Most breeders raise enough quail to meet orders that are placed. Taking pre-orders allows you to know the amount of quail you need to hatch out beforehand so you can prepare.

Make sure to check your state regulations regarding permitting if you consider any raising quail for dog training. There are different laws regarding releasing birds for dog training vs. hunting.

Eggs for reptiles

Snake and Monitor lizard owners can use quail eggs as a food source. For smaller snakes, the small Button quail egg is a good size (about the size of a nickel). For larger snakes a Coturnix egg would be good (just larger than a quarter). Certain snakes and lizards eat eggs in the wild and feeding eggs as part of a reptile's diet would be close to natural in a captive environment.

Some quail breeders that have breeding pairs can sell the eggs to reptile owners to directly feed the reptiles. You can provide the birds for the reptile owner to raise and keep and use the eggs his birds produce to use as feed for the reptiles.

Gourmet eggs

Coturnix quail eggs are considered a delicacy in restaurants. Quail eggs can be eaten any way you can eat a chicken egg. Pickled quail eggs are very popular. You can sell eggs for eating directly to the public at farmer's markets or from your farm or house. Talk with restaurant owners about supplying them directly with your quail eggs.

Some specialty stores will carry quail eggs. If you have a specialty store near you, talk with the owner and find out how they are getting their eggs supplied. You can offer them a better price or if they do not have eggs, talk about introducing some in the store. This can turn into a good customer for you if they find that their customers like and are buying the eggs.

Northern Bobwhite quail are popular hunting birds

Raising quail for restocking for hunting

Popular hunting preserves often will restock their property before hunting season starts. Different types of quail are hunted with the Northern Bobwhite quail being called the "Prince of Quails." You can provide quail to the preserves for restocking. You can keep breeding adults to collect the eggs and hatch out the chicks, pen raise them and then offer them to preserves. If you know of a breeder who sells chicks inexpensively, you can buy young chicks and pen raise them to offer to the preserves. You'll need to research how much preserves in your area are paying per bird and see if it is something you can make money with before investing in this venture.

Survivalists

Survivalists are people who are preparing or already prepared for disaster, emergencies or disruption of social order and governments. Survivalists often learn self-defense, stockpile food, and water, build structures such as fall-out shelters or survival retreats and prepare to be self-sufficient in the event of a catastrophe.

Quail are small and portable, do not require a large amount of space and produce a good sized egg for their size as well as being a good meat bird. They are easy to care for and reproduce quickly. They are an ideal animal for a survivalist to consider in the case of having to become self-sufficient.

In case of a bug-out (leaving the area) during a catastrophe, moving 8-10 quail would be something a survivalist could do. They could prepare a small moveable cage if needed to move out quickly. Once they have a base set up the quail could be moved to a larger, more permanent enclosure (possibly one that can be moved to allow them to scratch the ground up for bugs and edibles). The female quail will produce eggs just about every day as a daily food source.

You can supply quail to survivalists, or if you are a survivalist, you can look to quail to provide food for you or your family.

Chapter 10: More Ideas Specific to Ducks

Duck Near a Pond by Jeanne Boleyn

Build backyard duck ponds

People who live in urban areas may like to have some ducks. Ducks love water, so why not build a duck pond? There are thousands of ideas of how to build a duck pond. If you make yourself available to build a duck pond, you will need to discuss the home owner's ideas to come up with a plan.

To build a duck pond, find an area that has as little rocks as possible to make digging easier. Dig a pit the size and shape you want the pond to be. Taper the sides so it will go from shallow to deep rather than a drop off as ducks like to dabble at the pond edges.

Put in a plastic lining that is thick so it will not tear. Use large rocks to hold down the edges of the plastic around the pond. Arrange in as natural a way as possible. Put sand in using a clean sand around the pond.

Add aquatic plants like water lilies, and local fish, like koi, to the pond. The smaller the pond is, the more often you'll need to clean it. You can also put in a water filter to help keep the pond clean. When feeding fish, only give them enough to consume in 15 minutes to help keep the excess food from decaying in the water. Regularly clean out any fallen leaves or debris as it will rot in the pond and make it murky.

Some people might like a small fence around the pond to keep the ducks from wandering off. Materials can easily be found at any feed and supply store as well as the big box stores.

Waterfowl Hunting with a Poodle

Supplying Frozen ducks for training retrievers

Duck hunting using a retrieving dog is a popular sport. The retriever has to be taught how to retrieve, and part of that training is to use a duck carcass. Most hunters will buy a supply of frozen ducks and thaw them out as needed. The hunters need somewhere to buy their ducks, why not get them from you?

You'll need to have a place to raise your ducks if you plan to raise them from ducklings. Typically Mallards are the duck of choice. You may be able to buy immature ducks to supply to hunters and avoid the raising of ducklings. You would be the "middle man".

First do some research and find out if there is duck hunting in your area. If there is, is there enough of a market to get into this venture? If you can offer to ship in a special box that would open your market right up. Talk with local hunting groups as well as individual hunters and find out what they need. If you can supply it and make a profit- go for it.

Ducks to eat

The Pekin duck is the primary breed for duck meat today. It is considered a multi-purpose breed because it has a high production in egg laying. Muscovies are popular in some countries for their lean, red meat that is similar to beef. Indian Runners are at the top of the list for egg production as they can lay up to 345 eggs per year.

Ducks are processed at 6-7 weeks typically, and the processing of the duck is similar to that of chicken. The biggest market for ducks is the Asian market, but restaurants are starting to serve special duck dishes.

You can raise ducks for the meat market using the same avenues as you would a chicken. You can sell them from your farm if you can process them at your location, or you could sell them at Farmer's Markets to start.

Peking duck

Ducks for eggs

Duck eggs are rich in vitamins and are a particularly good source of vitamins A and D. The only vitamin not present in duck eggs is vitamin C. Duck eggs are also high in cholesterol, containing nearly twice the concentration of chicken eggs.

Duck eggs will stay fresher, longer due to their thicker shell. They also have more of the albumen (the clear part of the egg) making cakes and pastries fluffier and richer. More Omega 3 fatty acids are found in duck eggs. Omega 3 helps with brain health and healthy skin.

Another health benefit is for those with egg allergies. Most people who are allergic to chicken eggs can eat duck eggs without a reaction.

When comparing the duck egg to the chicken egg, you find 2x the Vitamin A, 6x the Vitamin D, and 2x the cholesterol. In general, all the vitamins in chicken eggs are found in higher concentrations in duck eggs.

You can do with a duck egg, everything you can do with a chicken egg. They can be poached, scrambled and used in baking. They make cakes rise higher due to the high fat content. Salted duck eggs are a popular Chinese recipe.

As with chicken eggs, there are many ways to sell your eggs. You can put up fliers in your neighborhood for local customers as well as bring your eggs to local Farmer's Markets. You can keep a log of buyers and offer them eggs on a regular basis from your farm.

Down Feather – Photo by Yoky

Ducks for Down

The layer of fine feathers found under the tougher outer feathers are the down feathers on a duck. Eider duck down is commercially the most widely used down. As a thermal insulator and as padding, down is the top choice for bedding (duvets), jackets, sleeping bags and pillows.

If you are processing birds for meat, the down of the bird is a by-product that you may find useful in making some extra money. You can sell the raw duck down online at sites like Ebay and Amazon or open a store on Etsy and sell your duck products.

Most down supplied from out of the country for products are plucked from live birds in horrific situations. Being able to sell a product where no animals were harmed during collection may be just the boost your product needs to bring in buyers.

###

In Conclusion

No matter if you have chickens, ducks or quail there is opportunity to make some money. You can make just enough to cover your feed, or if you are able to do many things well, you may be able to have a part or full time job with your birds. Try a few of the suggestions listed here. Some are challenging and some are just plain fun. Whatever you choose to do with your birds, the most important thing you can be doing with your birds is enjoying them.

About the Author

Tammie Cappuccio has been a New Englander and surrounded by animals all her life. With first a passion for horses, and then for birds, she has written over two dozen published articles and four books on those subjects to date. With her husband, Frank, and daughter Melyssa, they open their home to teenage foster children and incorporate the animals as therapy. As well as raising foster children, Tammie breeds and raises chickens, quail and finches and has an extensive collection of china horses.

,

www.ingramcontent.com/pod-product-compliance
Lightning Source LLC
Chambersburg PA
CBHW060418290526
45791CB00002B/806